Eyes Barely Above Water

By

Jillian S. M. Lurie

Dedicated to my Granddad Bob
for inspiring me to write

Book Playlist:
Calum Scott - Dancing On My Own
X Ambassadors - Unsteady
Bon Iver - Beach Baby
Cavetown - This Is Home
David Kushner - Burn
Rainbow Kitten Surprise - Devil Like Me
Xxxtentacion - Numb
Winter Aid - The Wisp Sings
Sparky Deathcap - September (We Got Fire)
Hozier - Eat Your Young
Between The Bars - Elliot Smith
ROS - Mac Miller
Caamp - By and By
Caamp - Misty
Bedroom - Move Forward
The Front Bottoms - "Cough It Out"
The Front Bottoms - "Swimming Pool"
The 1975 - Somebody Else
The 1975 - Robbers
The Front Bottoms - Twin Sized Mattress
Mr. Brightside - The Killers
The Doors - Alabama Song (Whiskey Bar)
Montell Fish - Destroy Myself Just For You
Clairo - Pretty Girl
Rhiannon - Fleetwood Mac
Fleetwood Mac - Dreams
Cage The Elephant - Shake Me Down
Pixies - Where Is My Mind?
Roar - I Can't Handle Change
Mac Miller - Stay
Mac Miller - Self Care
Mac Miller - Love Lost
Bedroom - In My Head

Mac Miller - Hand Me Downs
Billie Eilish - Everything I Wanted
Band Of Horses - The Funeral
Lizzie McAlpine - Ceilings
SZA - Broken Clocks
Mac Miller - Surf
The Cinematic Orchestra - 'To Build A Home'
Bon Iver - Holocene
Mazzy Star - Fade Into You
Lana Del Rey - Blue Jeans
Kodaline - All I Want (Part 1)
Angus and Julia Stone - Big Jet Plane
The Lumineers - Sleep On The Floor
Lana Del Rey - Ride
Hozier - From Eden
Bon Iver - Roslyn
Hozier - Cherry Wine
Gregory Alan Isakov - San Luis
Frank Ocean - White Ferrari
Montell Fish - Fall In Love With You
Gregory Alan Isakov - Big Black Car
Lana Del Rey - Video Games
Tom Odell - Another Love
Hozier - Work Song
Frank Ocean - Pink + White
Beach House - Space Song
Girl In Red - We Fell In Love In October
Bon Iver - Wash
Cage the Elephant - Cigarette Daydreams
Current Joys - Kids
Montell Fish - Love You More Than Me
Omar Apollo - Evergreen (You Didn't Deserve Me At All)
Frank Ocean - Ivy
SYML - Where Is My Love

Amy Winehouse - Back To Black
Harry Styles - Sign Of The Times
Post Malone - Feeling Whitney
Tash Sultana - Jungle
Blue Foundation - Eyes On Fire
Lykke Li - Little Bit
Gnarls Barkley - Crazy
Amy Winehouse - Valerie
Rainbow Kitten Surprise - Lady Lie
Ed Sheeran - The A Team
Adele - Hometown Glory
Coldplay - Yellow
The Lumineers - Salt And The Sea
The Lumineers - Ophelia
Guardin - I Think You're Really Cool
Henry Green - Electric Feel (Gespleu Downcast Edit)
(MGMT Cover)
FIDLAR - 40 oz. on repeat
Tracy Chapman - Fast Car
Grimes - Oblivion
Hippie Sabotage - Devil Eyes
Kate Bush - Running Up That Hill
The Cranberries - Linger
The Smiths - There's A Light That Never Goes Out
The Kooks - Naive
MGMT - Kids
The Killers - When You Were Young

It's so sad watching everyone around you die. It's so hard watching me love and live without you but with you it's like I so desperately want to shoot your soul and energy out of me. Just to breathe again into your grave and dig you out and bring you back to life. Jesus did it right. You're so alive baby girl-you're so alive. I'm so mad how can I fucking sleep when you're the only thing on my mind at this time. I can feel you with me. I'm freaking out and I feel you everywhere I hear you in the walls tapping because I haven't slept in days. I know it's you speaking to me so I know I'm not crazy. The medium told me "it's hard to reach me when my energy is low." It's high now! That's why I know I can feel you. My sanity is fading away word by word. I'm noticing that you're here inside of me and in the room through strange cravings for food you like. Everything is a sign. What is happening to me? Wait I know, it is grief.

June 20, 2016 3:26 am

When I hear the birds sing at 3:55 am it's you.
When I hear tapping in the walls at 3:45 I know it's your long lanky fingers saying hello. When I hear cars swish after I say I love you I know I can only hear it because you're saying "I love you too". You want me to remember us driving in your car how fast did I fall for you? That's all I have left.
You're dead but you're everywhere.
A poem about grieving.

June 20, 2016 4:00 am

That gold dot in my photo is the moon outside your doors. It only appears this way once in 70 years.

June 20, 2016 9:43pm

I love hearing mini thunderstorms and the morning birds right before I sleep. Thank you. R.O.S by Mac Miller plays; it's the song that reminds me of her. It thunders "I love you too." I speak to her ghost. Absolutely helplessly under the influence.

June 21, 4:29am 2016

It's 5:19 am and I'm still thinking I just wanted to let you know that I'm okay. I wish I could just tell you that. I'm more than okay. I listened for signs of you as I smoked weed. I watched the sunrise on my back porch completely alone. I'll tell you more about it one day soon when I'm with you. Honestly it's the only thing I'm reflecting on. I'm giving myself reassurance for the situations I'm in because every day is a new day. When the message to the person a million miles away is waiting for you. Trust me I will come my friend. I will and you already know it. This whole time sometimes when I get too outside myself and busy I forget the quiet self. The one that's introverted. The one that's like the sunrise is part of me during the day during all the running around. The one I can never see you in the reflections of the world. Really because I'm too busy but you are too. Then when the sun sets I talk to you it gets fiery like the sunset. I'll catch your attention every day, I hope you are an angel who protects me. When it's night and all the fun is happening and we drift again. We still talk because I can and I will because my denial lingers. Then I'll be alone when the sun rises and that's when you get these God awful messages from me. Sometimes I write in a book I'm writing. I write to cope then I move on. Just like how I'm talking to you now, that's how I cope. What I was trying to say this whole time. I keep you alive with these words. I just didn't gather myself yet and listen to what the universe and all the heavens could give me. I wrote this in a whole two minute song. I feel like I could write to you for hours. I'm okay now, really everything is okay. I hope you awaken with a smile and know that I am the breaking dawn. Know that I am the part after the sunrise. Know that I am the part after when the morning begins for most people and throughout the day. I am the wind and throughout the sunset. I am the color to catch your attention. I am the night and fluency of it. The life and soul that has disappeared from me burst alive like it never had before. Now it's gone I still feel dead. I am beginning to understand now. I get why you ended your life on drugs. Why would you die for them? Why would you leave us behind? That's what hurts. Not what really hurts the most. Regardless, that definitely makes me bleed out sometimes. Now I have made myself sick trying to understand. I get it though I really do.

June 22, 2016 at 5:42 am

I think to myself what the hell literally what the hell is wrong with me? Then I know and it horrifies me.

June 27, 2016 5:18 am

I understand you. I understand how you died and why you did it. I now understand you held the secrets to everyone and everything. You were silenced. So you chose to be alone. Then beauty happened. It was only in your eyes. You saw something. Something beautiful in the universe. Then you died. Now you're alive and free more than ever. We can no longer touch you, feel your soft skin. It makes me cry.

June 28, 2016 3:44 pm

I write:

Everyone: Jill what the hell is wrong with you? You were done talking for today! You've overdone it this time! I can't be with you when you over do it! See can't you even see the car horn! Or can you not even see clearly enough for that?

Me: I'm sorry, I don't know.

June 28, 2016 8:17 pm

Everyone's claiming to be independent.
I wonder if I am spiraling out of control.
No, I'm perfectly fine, just chemical reactions in my
brain.
"It's what you have told me before," she told me in my
head while I listened to her favorite songs.

June 28th, 2016 8:33 pm

They all saw me fading away and no one said anything. I mean it's when I grieve I feel this way. I'm not dying, I'm very alive on drugs. Seven days seven nights every week I am alive and dead, that's what the painkillers claim. Also, it claimed beware of the overdose so I am not taking more. I'm spreading the word like everyone else right that's why we're apart but working together. It's no contract it's just facts. They say you hear angels but it's Mac Miller's voice at these times you feel alone very alone. I know too much already. It's like okay we don't have to go back out there.

June 28th, 2016 8:39 pm

Do we all poison ourselves? Yes, that's how a lot of us die. We can't fight the inevitable. Literally everyone's soul has spoken to you. When you're alone for what feels like the first time they really talk. Then you look up and think "hmm show me the world!" Someone told me that before. There's a fine line between dead while alive: you either cross it, break it, and survive or write about it and live.

June 28th 2016 9:07 pm

Saw the lights of heaven-it was my mom's car lights. Intoxicated again

June 28th, 2016 9:18 pm

Everyone told me to shut the fuck up so I did. She told me farewell and meant it.
I can't talk to anyone anymore.
I have no one left.

June 28th, 2016 9:25 pm

I feel psychotic.
I can hear my abuser screaming in my head.
He follows me around.
Lingers around corners and hides when I am not looking. It drives me insane.
There's skeletons in my closet everywhere I look. Everywhere in my mind.

June 28th, 2016 9:45 pm

They came back but "I'm sorry" does not cut it.

June 28th, 2016 10:40 pm

Yeah I know we've all had shit we've needed to sort out and rearrange ourselves. The speed is unreal. The speed is in your own head. Creating language only other people of the same frequency can understand.

I have been abused but I abused myself. There comes a point where I need to slow my thoughts and just think about you on my own. So I don't stay up odd hours and see ghosts in a bad way.

June 29th, 2016 2:09 am

We're all artists hungry for what we have to say. It's the balance between life and death. You either tune into it or try to listen to others. However; the others you run into are chosen by the unknown. So I built a wall and planted roses around it. With lots of thorns. Showing only what I allow others to see inside. No, I am not ready to face my fears again. My fears make no sense to me. My fear is really the unknowing. Why fear the unknown? Why fear anything?
Notes by a feen.

June 29th, 2016 2:37 am

When someone dies it's always half them half you that dies too. At the breaking point whenever that is.

You're everything to me and you're an angel now. You've been trying to tell me this. My entire life you've always been there, you're going to heal me through healing you.

We cure ourselves of whatever it is through art. Art is anything down to how we speak to people. Even through our own words that we can't speak.

My mother doesn't understand what I cannot speak. The unspoken things between her and I.

That only the quiet at the quiet can understand.

It's what everyone knows.

No one pays attention to it.

I know and I understand why he hurt me. I always will understand. It's not okay to hurt others. It's okay to leave others who cannot control themselves. I wish at the time I knew that.

June 29, 2016 10:29 pm

Everyone would rather desert me than stay with me when I have no one. When I'm alone I'm very alone. When my senses are high.

June 30th, 2016 9:00 pm

I have such a bad ache in my head.

I am making my brain and body worse.

I don't care, I just want to be happy.

I want to get back in my bed.

It is cold without you.

You are all around me I know.

Really I don't know what I've been thinking these last few days.

I wanted you to love me.

How I love you.

You did that's what I want to believe.

Now your time on earth has come and gone. For reasons I still cannot explain. For you have not told me yet my love. You are gone so I sit and wait for answers that may never come. You're gone and you never even told me what you were going through. I wouldn't have judged you.

I would've told you little darling that's beautiful. Pain in life is beautiful, you know it right?

You need to fucking stop before you die. That's what I would have pleaded before she ended her life. Or maybe it is a higher power. I truly think that we do not control these things.

July 1st, 2016 12:34 am

The only emotion I feel when I'm on pills is sadness. The emotion I feel when I'm sober is everything. The only emotion I feel when I'm high is happiness. I get why you died.
I do not need to use it anymore to figure out why. Regardless, it has consumed me to cope.

July 3rd, 2016 2:06 pm

My mind is left with a cold suppressed static feeling.
I don't know who it is that makes me feel this way
anymore. Is it the living, the dead, him or my body?
The mind loves to solve things.
The mind craves change.
The mind sometimes hurts when nothing's changed.
I hate that I have lost my mind possibly for an eternity.

July 5th, 2016 12:46 am

I need the love back that I had never gotten in the first place.

July 5th, 2016 7:05 am

I think I realized why I go for men who don't throw themselves at me. When the abuser didn't want me I wanted him.

I have been left in the dark for so long now.

He is gone.

I never got the satisfaction of what it felt like to be wanted by someone you were on your knees for. Therefore, every one night stand I want to last.

This happens when I don't know what real want feels like.

July 5th, 2016 7:09 am

Jillian S. M. Lurie

Different types of hearts:
The part of your heart you can only give to someone
once.
Some hearts look bare because the possessor sliced it
off with their sharpest knife.
If you're lucky you won't meet someone with a knife
you'll meet someone with a paint brush.
Knives cut things that can't grow back on their own.
Paint brushes create a mask over the blank slate.

July 5th, 2016 7:24 am

I don't like being alone.
I wish he were here with me.
With promise he might call back.
I don't like false hope.
I want his touch.
Didn't you tell me not to give a man the time of day if
he was bothering me? I wish I could ask.
What I could do to him?
What I haven't done?

July 5th, 2016 5:08 pm

The life was eating you whole wasn't it. Your veins were tight with fear and rage. Thought you were in control.
You weren't.
My fist just clenches.
It was all in your head.
Until it wasn't.
I just want to escape from myself.

July 6th, 2016 12:16 am

You aren't forced to fend for yourself.
You just simply want to.
When there's nothing happening.
Just the survival mode I presume.
You're aware of the revolutions you find on the road.
Not like the traveler.
More like the seller.
Until you strike gold in all your fear.
Just think about it.

July 6th, 2016 1:34 am

You think you can stop everything then control it again.
It's a pattern of messing with too many people.
It's not nothing.
There's just energy everywhere.
Hoping one day that you can make something out of it.
Just like everyone hopes.
You are just growing up.
The point in which you decide who's a bad man and who's not. When your thoughts don't become yours anymore.
They become everyone around you.
You think people want to hear what you have to say.
These are dangerous thoughts. These treacherous thoughts in the dark. When the wall is cracking.
It's not the drugs.
It's your mind I could have sworn it is.
Working on everything around you.
People ask, "are you okay?"
You say, "yeah, I'm just sober."
We all have things that are valid and invalid.
Everything everyone does is valid.
Everyone's so scared.
Masked by confidence.
Created on the drugs you have taken when you were young.
These are the mistakes of humanity.
These we cannot control.
These I cannot control at least.
Maybe not now, not yet I have had too much.

July 6th, 2016 2:06 am

I wish my words couldn't hurt another. Why do I have that power? Why can't they just go away? No one can see the depths of me. It's like my life to others is invisible. That is fine. I want to be invisible a lot. I can't speak when the wonders of everyone's trip is blurring your own dreams. I wonder why I am growing up in a heartless city.

August 4, 2016 10:54 am

Addictions to alcohol are fun.
Spit on ones you love.
While they tell you life is important.
Pretending life is not important is easier.
Downers rise as uppers.
My love is wilted.
Oblivious oblivion regained.

August 4th, 2016 11:23 am

Something inside my chest screams I hate you.
Something inside my chest screams forgiveness.
My inner energy dies beneath my breasts.

August 15th, 2016 10:30 pm

"I hate myself."
As a "friend."
As a "lover."

August 20th, 2016 3:08 pm

She
She is connected to women, not men.
She is the energy I breathe around me. She is independent and free of will. She is the spirit that has transcended.

August 29th, 2016 4:19 pm

Fear is love.
Love is dying.
Love is crying.
Love is wondering if they'd want to stay. Love is harm and worry.
My heart is an open field. My love is deep.
My love is valued.
I don't fear.
-being in love with the devil vs an angel.

September 3rd, 2016 11:29 pm

My thoughts go from I don't want anyone.
I want him.
I'm so close to the blossom of my life.
How should I know who I want to grow from? Where
I want to plant my seeds.
So many men could water my garden.
And stomp on my roses.
But more would rather smell me.
Don't want the oils of their skin to damage my surface.

September 5th, 2016 12:28 pm

She goes through me like the ocean shallow at the surface. The moon makes her stronger as it blooms off the sun.
I miss you, my little darling.
You flood my bones.

September 6th, 2016 6:10 pm

From miles away he shot me a smile.
I understood what love and commitment meant. Loving
without touching.
Long distance relationships.

September 6th, 2016 11:56 pm

Betrayal is what you can see when you're blinded for so long. How a dark soul craves light.
Only to diminish it.
Protecting myself is the only thing I know.
I just hate feeling alone in the dark tunnel.
I see fire that is my soul at the end.
Mostly light of day.
Leaving the ones I love was never hard for me. I'd been living with a heart of fear.
I do wonder if you can tear those walls down with the creativity of your eyes. Wide and brown deeper than me.

September 12th, 2016 1:45 pm

I just want to die because she's dead.
I am ashamed of my actions and what others see in my reflection.

September 12th, 2016 1:53 pm

As darkness formed around her, I pretended not to care.
I did not want to upset anyone.
God forbid anyone I loved was upset with me.
Is that a trauma response?

September 15th, 2016 8:31 pm

Never let your soul below the flesh sink into the dark forever. Even if darkness tries to swallow your light. That is the darkness's job, just don't let it work for you.

September 16th, 2016 2:41 am

Jillian S. M. Lurie

The heart breaks.
If you survive through the pain.
There's a phase of being numb.
Then it heals, leaving you bitter.
At least you can feel it beating. Reminding the soul it
is okay to be alive. Even when you are not.

September 17th, 2016 7:07 pm

I want the world to stop because it stopped you. You are dead and gone.
The world killed you.
It is killing me.

September 18th, 2016 1:27 am

Forty two times I tried to die.
Every time I saw the white light, I decided there was more.
Every time I just needed to do more.
I didn't want that.
I wanted more.
You learn to live for the ones you love.
That is what the meaning of okay is.
I mean just look at the way people laugh around you.
That within itself is a reason to live.
Just the pure serendipity of a smile meeting a laugh is the single most beautiful painting in the world.

September 20th, 2016 9:05 pm

Times are always changing but I'll be alright. I mean that is what they say. "I just want someone to tell me it won't be alright. That is how I feel. That is not what I am used to. Things are just alright. I mean how do people even know that? For me, for my fate." I muttered to myself with tears in my eyes.

September 20th, 2016 9:59 pm

I don't hurt the same.
My mind twists and turns. Feeling my stomach be numb. My jaw clenched.
The flowers of my being wilted. I am now my past. Living in the future.
That is my ptsd for you.

October 5th, 2016 10:43 pm

Am I too young to know what I really want?
I feel like a loner.
I feel like no one wants what I have to offer.
I am a burden to others because the weight on their shoulders is too unbearable.
I say powerful words I wish others could say to me.

It's like I give until I have nothing but confusion.
No one really stays.
I wonder what they say behind closed doors.
I miss her and the reassurance she gave me.

I never felt like less of a person when looking into her brown eyes.

October 6th, 2016 3:00 am

I looked over at her, she was careless. I craved that.

October 6th, 2016 11:27 pm

All the tears I hold back, Why?
I'm angry I'm not sad,
My best friend is now bones, So move on?
I am expected to just move on?
It's not easy.
She could be alive but she's not.
She took a whole part of me with her.
Everything I didn't know she knew.
I'm hoping that when I see you again it will be beautiful.
I hate the fact I need to live a whole life without your presence. How the fuck could a heart like yours do that to me?

October 11th, 2016 1:00 am

One time I cried myself to sleep. My mom took a Post-It note and wrote on it:
"You may never know.
Just how much.
You are loved."
I love her so much for that. When I woke up it was right there. I will never forget it. It is almost poetic.

November 2nd, 2016 5:06 pm

I urged him to come silently.
I wondered about my worth.
Knew exactly what it was to him.
Maybe absolutely nothing.
He was a ghost to me.
He's never going to come back.
My love has disappeared.
The pain is a numbness in the absence of my lover.

August 14th, 2017 9:49 pm

If only you let my love flourish.
If only you sat under the sun and watched me grow.
If only I knew how to make you stay.

September 2nd, 2017 1:46 am

Sometimes you must sit. Swallow your pride.
And let your loneliness reside.

September 28th, 2017 2:16 am

Jillian S. M. Lurie

Everyone owns their own pain
Only few can cut the petals off
Begin to grow and flourish once more. -growing

September 29th, 2017 9:11 pm

They all want a slice of you. Only all the wrong pieces.

September 30th, 2017 12:40 pm

I miss that one person who stopped at nothing to make sure I was loved.

October 5th, 2017 1:42 pm

Someone questioned me, "why aren't you falling in love again?"

"Fear." I relayed and shrugged.

But my heart willed to me: "it's because I belong to someone already."

October 7th, 2017 6:03 pm

For weeks I tried to understand why you'd hurt me so bad.
I still don't have an answer.
As long as we're apart it stings more.
My broken heart feels like he held my heart in his hands and poured salt in it.
Trying to convince myself that it will be okay through all of it.
However your words and your actions linger through every person I meet.

October 12th, 2017 1:33 pm

It was your warmth I desired.
I meant what I said when I didn't want anyone else to touch me like you did. I'm distant because my heart belongs to you.
No soul can have me like you do.
I'm grieving for someone so alive.
Someone who's forgotten what our love feels like.
Love and heartbreak.

October 13th, 2017 1:45 am

I only hate him because I'm trying to forget. The more I try to forget the more I remember.

October 13th, 2017 3:00 am

Make me at least your sweetest regret, you are mine.

October 13th, 2017 4:45 am

You taught me more about love than I've ever known. You also taught me more about pain as well so much so that I'll never feel it again. Only because I actually loved you.

October 13th, 2017 5:09 am

My tears feel hot with rage.
Over losing what I once had.
Inventing
I should reinvent myself right? I'm changing without
you.
See me grow!
I wish you stood at my doorstep.
Tell me you regret it.
Losing me was a mistake.
You can't see that, blind.

October 17th, 8:59 am

Jillian S. M. Lurie

There's a hole in my heart you created. Only to be filled by my own love.

October 20th, 2017 8:52 pm

He told me I was beautiful.
At that moment it felt like the first time I heard it. I am beautiful.

December 17th, 2017 4:30 pm

I want to matter to someone like how I matter to you because since you've been gone no one has.

January 25th, 2018 8:00 pm

I want to be perfect, not perfect like her. Perfect within me. Acceptance.

March 18th, 2018 9:58 pm

Jillian S. M. Lurie

I would give anything to get out of this life. Get out of
this life with no more karma.
So that I wouldn't give anything for the next.

April 12th, 2018 1:04 pm

Sometimes I hide from kindness.

July 16th, 2018 2:43 pm

And just like that I force myself to be able to love again.
J

July 24th, 2018 2:08 pm

I noticed your imperfections.
Imperfections I will soon come to love one day.

September 7th, 2018 10:52 am

I knew that if I stayed.
My reality would tear me.

November 8th, 2018 10:07 am

I'm where I need to be right now and that's okay.

November 28th, 2018 9:20 pm

Therapist: why not just choose love? Why not just give someone a chance again?

Myself: the heartbreak was cold when he left me. I wanted time to freeze because I didn't want to go on without her. It was frustrating at the time and still is. As much as my heart longs for a lover I never want time to freeze again. I feel as if maybe it is not worth the risk. I do not feel safe.

December 3rd, 2018 8:59 am

Letting go actually feels okay. I might feel comfortable in this space for a while. I might just stay in this energy-walk around see how it feels. Move in maybe.

December 5th, 2018 7:45 pm

As the hole in my chest forms once more.
The face I adored.
I'm missing once more.
I am lightning that is silent yet storming and electric.
All at once.
Also very powerful energetically. Everyone is powerful energetically. Just not everyone knows it yet.

December 7th, 2018 1:41am

There's strength in trees.
The roots of their souls digs deep.
They capture the dark cold earth and make a fist.

December 7th, 2018 1:54 am

Abuse

Forgetting things is so prominent. I was forced to forget about the wrong, however sometimes the skeletons haunt me. They stick

to my soul even in his absence. It begs the question. How could something so heinous happen to someone that wouldn't hurt a fly?

March 18th, 2019 11:54 pm

I thought I could replace you.

April 13th, 2019 8:24 pm

Thank you for teaching me how to be numb when needed, babe. I appreciate it. If we never broke up I would have never known.

April 14th, 2019 12:21 pm

I want to say I'm over you.
I want it bad so bad I'd do anything.
Sometimes I feel like I have been over you.
I really believe I am.
Unfortunately, I'm not.
If I saw you at my doorway I'd run to the door to open it.
Greet you with that wide smile you taught me.
Melt with tears of joy.
Kiss you.
Hug you tightly and not let go.
I would cherish your scent as my joyful tears hit your shirt.
I would invite you in and be grateful.
That's what makes me feel like I'm just never going to be able to make it all the way over you. -self arguments.

April 16th, 2019 10:55 am

I sat and waited for your arrival but you've never returned my heart.

April 26th, 2019 11:12 am

I sat here in the morning remembering the peace I felt when I was with you.
Nothing was ever not okay. It was strange, it wasn't real. Perhaps that is why it ended.

May 9th, 2019 9:16 am

Tonight's thoughts:
I hate your existence without me.
My focus has shifted to how I can possibly see you.
Old warm parts of my heart I need back are burning with desire.
I'm a joke. You don't notice me.
I fear your friends will change my fate.
No one should have that right.
I can feel myself shattering slowly this time.
I'm aware it's going to be worse beyond my control like cutting at an old scar.
My heart and body looks for a home within others now.
I suffocated you while I looked to catch my breath from the outcome.
I feel pure shame now.
You humiliated me.
He doesn't understand he never will.
Hold me hold me again.

May 10th, 2019 12:53 am

We stand in front of the mirror like actors.
We act out situations we are most weary of. However, nothing is ever expected or predicted. This leaves us speechless.
I just lay on the floor and cry.

May 19th, 2019 9:22 pm

Let it drown.
It's ok to melt it.
Move along.

May 20th, 2019 12:09 am

Good to know I was nothing.
No big deal.
Not hard to get over.
Not a single bone in your body cared enough to try for me or cry for me. My love wasn't worthy I suppose.
No heartache.
I was so effortlessly taken for granted nothing but a shrug of pain for you to be over us. Maybe my immense pain was so powerful you didn't need to carry it too.
You told me you got me. You lied about that.
I told you I got you. I would never give someone my word and lie about it.
I'm torn and meaningless.

May 26th, 2019 11:53 am

He puzzled me.
Relearning that it was wrong.

May 28th, 2019 11:45 pm

Flustered is the emotion.
You were everything I wanted.
Now you're everything I want and more. Your absence
makes me poor.

May 29th, 2019 10:32 pm

My heart is reaching, I can feel it again. It came back
to me this morning!
What a miracle I can feel it again.

May 29th, 2019 10:58 pm

I can't stop picturing my life with you.
It was a promise I kept.
My heart needs to accept what my mind already knows.
It leaves me fickle.

June 1st, 2019 1:29 am

I am a beautiful flower. I am wilting.

June 1st, 2019 11:26 pm

Is it getting bad again, do I know?
Will I relapse?
Or will it reveal itself at my worst?
Will my temporary happiness be nothing but that?
Paranoid chats with myself.

June 1st, 2019 11:30 pm

My heart is singing again. My flower.

June 2nd, 2019 6:00 am

Who am I trying to convince? Myself?

June 13th, 2019 12:39 pm

My mind uses a stress ball.
To comfort and erase pain and knowledge.
Every time I squeeze it daggers come out and stab my hand. Why do I try?
Why do I ask that question when I already know my answer. No one else can understand.

June 13th, 2019 11:49 pm

I love you,
Goodnight.
An unsent message.

June 16th, 2019 9:11 pm

Talk to me please.
Talk to me.

June 17th, 2019 12:58 am

Speak to me with music.

June 18th, 2019 2:08 am

Let me grab you.
Pull me in by my thighs.

June 18th, 2019 2:35 am

I need to live my life.
I'm not meant for right here.

June 18th, 2019 2:39 am

eu·pho·ri·a
/yo͞o'fôrēə/
a feeling or state of intense excitement and happiness.
● you.

June 18th, 2019 2:42 am

I don't deserve to be here.
Definitely not instead of her.
Why did that even happen?
I just find myself searching for these answers over and
over again.
In the midst of searching I only find new questions that
tear me up over tears.

June 18th, 2019 11:13 am

I'm isolating.
Why am I melting inside of myself? Only my heart knows the answer to that. My heart has been in my hands.
I gave it away.

June 24th, 2019 11:15 pm

I like having no one know who I am.
-protection.

June 29th, 2019 10:35 pm

Would you make that mistake again?
Yes, definitely.

June 30th, 2019 5:27 pm

Only we understand and accept. I intend to keep it that way.

July 4th, 2019 10:46 am

Joy,
You are a waterfall.
One that flows heavily as I stand beneath. I cannot catch you.
Nor can I fathom your beauty.
You bring tears to my eyes.

July 6th, 2019 4:13 am

I've planned this day.
I've known what I've wanted to say and do for two years. If I ever got the chance to embrace you once more.
Only   now   I'm   speechless.
Please stay forever with me.

July 10th, 2019 2:10 pm

Hold me with my face on your chest by your heart.
Hold me a long time and rub my head after kissing it.
Squeeze me tighter.
As I listen to my entire body relax in your presence. -
All I crave.

July 11th, 2019 11:48 am

Love and self-harm is a fine line for me.

July 12th, 2019 8:17 pm

Don't forget to remember what made you lose him.
Don't forget to remember all the flaws that he made you aware of.
Don't forget to remember you can't lose him again.

July 20th, 2019 2:01 am

Please hold true to our last night together.
Please hold true to only the good things.
One last time.

July 25th, 2019 8:39 pm

When I thought of us I thought we're going to last forever. Such a dangerous thought.
-Anxiety

July 28th, 2019 9:03 pm

You are the ocean that overcomes me.

Most of it is not discovered.

As beautiful as it is, there are monsters in that sea.

I could drown.

You have killed me before.

You didn't love me enough to protect me from the danger around me. It took me too long to realize that I shouldn't love people like that. No matter how perfect they make it feel.

You need to protect people that you love.

There are monsters in the water.

You will drown if you do not tread lightly.

August 3rd, 2019 12:55 am

Find me over the mountains. I want nothing more.

August 3rd, 2019 12:55 am

I want him to feel every part of me. Desire to touch
my energy.
Kiss me like you mean it.
Fall in love with me.

August 4th, 2019 5:55 pm

Hidden skeletons in the closet.
Peer out at me as I look at the open graveyard of my skeletons.

August 5th, 2019 7:45 pm

I'm certain I want to be hypnotized and forget who you are. It's the only way to forget. However, furthermore, I would be ripping away so much of who I am when I look at you. I see nothing in your eyes and the eyes are the windows to the soul.

August 6th, 2019 7:09 pm

I am a botanist of my own mind. Please water my flowers.
I want an endless grasp of my roses. Please don't make me touch my thorns.

August 8th, 2019 1:11 pm

"Don't let it become me!" I argue with myself. "It already is coming." I argue back.

August 9th, 2019 1:48 am

Every time my perception of his perception of me comes to my mind it still drags me through the mud.

It's like this made up perception wants me to change things I love about myself.

I think his opinion wants to change this about me. Then my small voice whispers but I like that about myself.

Never let anyone decide what's not to love. Love is great.

Success is a hard weight to pick up, hold, and carry.

Loving myself is holding a whole boulder over my head. While just barely keeping it up while proud I'm standing, not everyone can. At least I can finally just say that. It is hard but I finally have self-love.

August 9th, 2019 1:50 am

I'm beginning to realize my self-love through fighting with him on the inside of my body.

Fighting not to change. I don't want to appease him. Regardless of how powerful the urge to be who I think he wants me to be is. I realize now, no. I don't want to change that I never don't want to be who I am. I am more than okay with who I am.

I'm starting to realize tendencies and realizations about my mental health, not ready to write it down or say out loud because I could never tell anyone only myself.

- • self protection technique right there and symptoms of paranoia through trauma.
- • That's a fresh realization.
- • It bleeds through my writing and makes me self conscious.
- • I hide.
- • I fear.
- • I fear not being accepted and I can't say why.
- • I can't even write it down, insane to me the slim chance someone would find it.

August 9th, 2019 1:56 am

My mind is a puppeteer.
My body is a puppet on strings.

August 9th, 2019 2:40 am

The moments you are sleeping. Wondering what to think.

Wondering what it is.

Wondering what it is that's confusing me. However, I do know.

I've dreamt of this and wanted this for two whole years.

Is this what I've been yearning for?

I feel weakened by your withdrawal.

Do I believe you'll be here in a better way for me? After all this I just lay here observing, hoping our bodies will intertwine. He told me that was forbidden after embracing me for three whole days.

I get it she's new, fresh and exciting.

Is she really?

I wondered this morning contemplating how I should be like her as if I know who she is.

I feel like I've gone mad.

I can't put a name on feelings that all come as one together: the good, the bad, the normal emotions, and the romantic all at once. In this specific way there's not a single word to describe it.

In other words, I relapsed. I knew she did drugs and so did he. It was all around me, So I relapsed, I wanted to look appealing.

I thought about how normal she must be. How different and weird I was. Maybe she was outrageously filled with energy. I was calm. I was really slow and peaceful. Maybe he just liked that she wasn't like me at all. Envy made me relapse too. I felt ashamed.

I couldn't stop thinking about what toxins he allows in his life through people.

I'd love to think that's part of my rejection but it's not it's me it's her.

So I relapsed. The pills stared me in the face over and over again. I was not strong enough.

He's quiet, I would love to think it's because it's who he is.

I can't help but think it's significant to only me. I had a vague memory of when we used to date and he used to talk all the time. So him not talking to me made me paranoid. Maybe it's my anxiety that convinces myself of these things. Expect the unexpected.

Is this a long lost romance? Yes. Will this be the end? I can't say.

I wonder how she's gonna hurt you? I wonder how sad it's gonna be when you vent about it and I have to say I told you to protect yourself.

I am suddenly realizing I'm connected to the person who stole my heart, didn't take care of it, and let it wither away while damaging me an embarrassing amount. Meanwhile, he does not have a care in the world. All while I'm here. Confused but not confused at all.

To figure out just how much I can be capable of.

What he's capable of? Maybe rewire my brain to be like her or better than her? Maybe I'll have the guts to ask him how do you love him so much then not at all? How can you go into a relationship months after leaving someone? Someone that you've considered spending your life with? It really makes me wonder just how much the girl is worth because maybe he's just filling voids. He may be getting excited when it's enabled and at all costs will fill it immediately.

Where does that leave us? Leaving us behind?

Building a future friendship?

Giving me what I've always wanted?

No, I'm not sure but I want my one last time to be conscious of it. I'm grateful and amazed we'd hold each other and he wouldn't want to let me go. You say you want her but you hold me at night. You tell me you don't want me and you hold me at night.

Hear me when I say I'm scared. I came miles to visit you then you just disappear for hours to go see her. It's ok. I have your drugs.

I wish you wanted to at least run one finger down my spine. Your energy soothes my chakras and my brain will be at peace.

How awkward am I? Answer: that's a trick question. Both are responsible. His silence makes me struggle. My nervous mind has been taking control a lot. I hate this. However, he said everything is okay. That I shouldn't care because he's fine. Okay I guess.

I wonder if today, currently at 1:38 pm, will be the day I've been hoping for. The day I hate this man and I am over it.

Once in a lifetime.

I feel like he's a mountain of sand and I'm struggling to get to the top. That is truly what it feels like trying to talk to this man.

Will I ever see him again? So much will happen in between. He'd move on so will I. What is it all worth? Who cares even?

Maybe our lives had to come together at this moment because we're supposed to be in each other's lives in the future. Only when we aren't lost. Imagine feeling that at the same time.

A hopeless romantic becomes me. It warps my body. I look over at him peacefully sleeping and sigh. I looked to the moon.

August 9th, 2019 1:40 pm

It's okay. It's okay. It's okay! It's okay. Okay. Okay!
Fine!
It's fine.
Fine.
Fine!
Fine!
It's Fine.
It's Fine!
It's Fine.
All with different meanings. All can be used in powerful lies.

August 9th, 2019 6:16 pm

I wonder if he's trying not to care.
"Yes" I thought to myself.
"Now stop wondering" I thought to myself.

August 9th, 2019 at 6:17 pm

"I'm fine"
Are we both lying?

August 9th, 2019 at 6:18 pm

"I love you."
I think to myself:
"why?"

August 9th, 2019 7:20 pm

What bothers me deeply is my lack to even try to be perfect. I never try with my looks.

I don't try to be conservative I am raunchy in my humor.

I smoke cigarettes and I used to do drugs for fun.

I search for thrill in life instead of simplicity.

I enjoy taboo opinions. I have taboo opinions.

I don't mind the company of addicts. Or the company of people losing their minds. I am just not normal. As a result people feel comfortable around me. I have heard so many strangers' wildest secrets over a cigarette. I almost think I cannot quit because of it. I definitely never try for a perfect temperament. Not in an angry way. I don't lash out at people. I am pretty anxious and broken. My personality is absolutely not perfect, I just don't care for it to be. Is that bad? I am far too honest. People are used to liars.

I don't care to have hobbies so that doesn't lead me to a perfect life.

I even eat leftover cake for breakfast when no one can see.

So on and so forth.

Make a checklist of imperfect things, I have done them.

Why even try if I could never compare to her.

I can't stop thinking he appreciates me less. Treats me as lesser. He is changing the way he treats me. Only because she's the only thing in his eyes. Why even try if I'm unchangeably perceived as lesser?

Just leave my mind. Make me hate you.

August 10th, 2019 1:02 am

He runs from me.
Even in his dreams.
I want to wrap myself around him when I try. He moves away from me.
Then gets close to me.
All subconsciously.

August 10th, 2019 4:21 am

"How am I supposed to um."
"How am I supposed to?" I gasp.
"How am I supposed to fix us?"
"How am I supposed to move on when it's this easy to get over me."

August 11th, 2019 8:47 am

Really, you want me back to see you, you care? "Yes."
You're lying to me, why are you lying to me?
I scream inside with dismay.
I wanted him to argue his point.

August 11th, 2019 9:06 am

I hold a torch through an unknown pitch black hall.
I can see darkness in front of me.
Fear to look around for things beside me.
With a phobia of being chased by the harm of the past
so I don't look backwards.
So I pause, freeze and gain courage to come forward.
Where is my courage?

August 11th, 2019 10:34 am

I don't need to travel 2538 miles to find that. I am home within myself.
I can get what's around more.

August 15th, 2019 1:57 am

Jillian S. M. Lurie

I make a hard effort to dust my mind until it's clear. I
always miss a spot.
That spot is always you.
I need to find that place you live in my mind.
So I can erase you for good.

August 17th, 2019 8:40 pm

I make a hard effort to dust my mind until it's clear. I always miss a spot.
That spot is always you.
I need to find that place you live in my mind.
So I can erase you for good.

August 17th, 2019   8:40 pm

Absence. Is that becoming us again?
No matter how it came true at least I got my wish.

August 17th, 2019 11:56 pm

My hands reach to hold up sand dunes.
Grasping the fine sand, watching it slide through my
fingers and fall into the abyss.
You are sand.

August 18th, 2019 1:22 am

My efforts are ignored.
I'm powerless.
It's almost my time to go.
Maybe never come back.
Forever doesn't exist anymore.
He promised me he wouldn't leave. I hate getting lied
to.

August 18th, 2019 1:31 am

You're ignoring me. Why are you ignoring me? Why am I fucking shocked?

August 18th, 2019 at 3:04 am

How many cigarettes do I have left that I cry over you with?

August 18th, 2019 3:06 am

So this is where our story ends.

There will be no other time I'll ask about his life.

I don't care anymore.

No other time will I try to be in it.

When I move across the country I'm going to pretend my past was normal. Everything will be skeletons in the closet.

Anyone who asks if I have mental problems I have none.

I'll talk about my day or what other people talk about.

I'm never talking about my pain no one will know.

I'll live the untouched, undamaged life I've always dreamed of.

How should I push this behind me and move on?

I need to ask my therapist because this can't haunt me. He doesn't care.

I need to match that I'm so relaxed I am moving on.

I have no need for someone that pathetic around.

Clearly he doesn't need me either. Healthy people are strangers to him.

September 1st, 2019 2:51 pm

Jillian S. M. Lurie

what's fucking wrong with me?
I only saw what I wanted to see.
This whole time it was like a classic case of not
knowing him at all.

September 2nd, 2019 1:14 am

Sometimes we don't quite know exactly why.
We do what we do.
We just do it because we enjoy it.
We live.
Then we die.

September 2nd, 2019 11:29 pm

Waiting for that one person who makes me feel like every other man doesn't exist.

September 4th, 2019 12:47 pm

I wonder if you miss me.
I wonder why I wonder.
Just kidding, I know why.

September 7th, 2019 11:54 pm

Nobody gets to know me.
I know me.
I love me.
Nobody deserves to know me anymore.

September 18th, 2019 2:19 pm

My life slips away from me like waves returning to a deep sea of the unknown.
I am getting older.

September 28th, 2019 10:49 pm

I'm not happy with the tragedies that have happened to me. I'm happy with who I am because of it. He can't take that from me.

October 13th, 2019 1:58 am

You tear me while you're untorn. How do I not let that happen anymore.

October 13th, 2019 2:02 am

I wish I could die.
I wish it was a lot easier to die.

October 15th, 2019 3:57 pm

Contemplating suicide hurts more than the commission.

October 16th, 2019 1:53 am

My world has no boundaries for the unexpected to happen.

October 17th, 2019 1:31 pm

I'm sick of the constant anxious thoughts going through my head every night. I need medication but I refuse to poison my body. I refuse to take drugs again. I just wish I didn't have a grudge against anxiety medication. I feel as if dealing with my anxiety without medicine builds character. Seeing that it has destroyed so many of my old friends' lives. Forcing me to leave them. Pills changed who they were. Not in a good way. Forcing me into the position that I can't talk to them anymore. People I knew my whole life just turned into horrible evil people. I couldn't risk doing pills because of this. Or they did something under the influence to hurt me indirectly or directly. Not to mention all the stolen lives of those addicted to pills and drugs. I don't wish the same fate for me. Just knowing how they're addictive and worsen your anxiety too. It doesn't help the thought of medical treatment either. That being said I know these work for people who moderate them well. I would just rather have holistic medicine. Anxiety meds are not for everyone, myself included.

December 4th, 2019 12:11 am

Here I am at 2:36am living despite it all.
Listening to the rain fall as I lie wide awake.
In an unknown place.
In a new phase of my life.
December is the end of all chapters.
Every year new details and stories.
I feel alone even when surrounded.
"Why is this?" I ask myself.
Well it's really because life leaves me hollow.
Everything I've loved gets ripped away from under me and it feels like an earthquake in my chest.
I can't shake some things happening.
Nonetheless, I sure as hell can try.
I hope to get some sleep tonight.
Focusing on the rain, the warmth of the sheets which some people don't have. I count my blessings carefully.
Grounding.
Grounding in a life with no grasp.

December 14th, 2019 2:36 am

I need to trust myself and do what's right.
Hopefully, this coming year will bring me kindness and joy. Hopefully, I'll have success.
Hopefully, my dreams will come true.
My world this year as I know it broke down.
My life is so challenging.
Trying to get a grasp on it is like holding onto sand in the wind. Sometimes you can't control it.
It is what it is and maybe that's ok.

December 14th, 2019 2:49 pm

Being alone protects me from harm.

December 14th, 2019 2:51 pm

Drinking alone.
Conscious mind: sigh he must've thought I was mental
like who knows what he could think of me.
Alcohol: it's fine.
Me: thanks, you're right, move on.
Excuse me, can I have some more wine?

December 23rd, 2019 2:15 am

I feel like a stranger to my own life.

December 23rd, 2019 4:38 pm

Five years six years seven years four three even one.
All the years just warped away.
Gone.
Leaving me in the moment with a new year on the rise.
What dismay will it bring?
What happiness?
What tragedy?
I feel lately a part of me is missing.
Perhaps a new me is on the rise.

December 23rd, 2019 4:54 pm

I remember being here with her body.
I remember the warmth she brought to my energy.
She's a ghost now.
Sometimes I wonder how that's actually possible. She was a part of life.
Time slips away without her.
Life is unfair.

December 23rd, 2019 4:56 pm

So many lives around me.
I wonder which is the saddest.
Is it me?

December 23rd, 2019   4:59 pm

We need to defy all odds.
We need to leave earth and start all over again.

February 12th, 2020 4:27 am

I find comfort in being alone.
It's not always lonely, I am always with myself.
I'm not empty anymore.
I'm trying to live functionally again.
I feel like everything is so peaceful and bare in the moment just gliding through life.
I'm comfortable being single.
It's a safe place to be alone.
No threat that they might be all there or not.
It's comfortable here.
I'm too vulnerable in a relationship.
It makes me fragile.
If someone made me comfortable and was confident in me maybe. just maybe it'll work.

February 12th, 2020 1:29 pm

Suddenly I only want you.
I whispered to you in your sleep.

March 18th, 2020 7:12 pm

I look over to old lovers in the distance. Will I ever know this?

March 22nd, 2020 9:43 pm

Jillian S. M. Lurie

Will they love my mind inside my bones?
As well as the words that go through my body?
All to connect with loving them.

March 22, 2020 11:19 pm

How many moons will it take to get to my lover? I need him now.

Every time I think I'm right I'm wrong.

I'm losing trust within myself to find you.

I hope that doesn't make me miss a chance of knowing you. Who do I even deserve?

March 23, 2020 9:55 am

My departure from my dark past is soon.
What will I say to the one that got away.
Should I ask him if I would ever be his girl?
Then stay if he says yes.
However, I know he doesn't care for me in that way.
How should I tell him?
Sometimes I look at him and get sad that I have to go.
Sometimes I profess my love to him in his sleep.
I wish my life could stop for him but it won't.
I have to leave my life and be willing to do so.
It's crazy how we bloom together only to wilt and fade away. It will hurt seeing him not care at all after an entire year.
I wonder what it has to say about me.
I wonder if I'm unlovable right now.
I guess not everyone is like that though.
Everyone falls differently for different types of people.
I guess I'm just a body to most of them.

December 29th, 2020 9:45 am

It's insulting after a year of dating this person he doesn't love me or care. Is that what it is for me-unloved and unseen? As someone who you shouldn't care for romantically, why is there a theme in my life? Why I do care if who I lay with cares. What's wrong with me? Should I hide the parts I love about myself to be loved? So when I'm unloved I won't take it personally?

January 8th, 2021 1:43 am

There comes time in your life when you reflect. I thought I was happy until I realized I cannot predict the future. My mistakes I made. I thought I could have shown up lately. I want to leave and have a family and a good job. Maybe my life is defeating me because it's meant to have me stuck here. I'm suffering and spiraling. I wish I played my cards right. I suppose I haven't had all my plans. I don't feel like trying to make anything work anymore because nothing has. I can't say if it ever will.

Everyone looks so happy and put together then there's me.

January 8th, 2021 7:02 pm

Stillness of a cold winter night outside is like you're experiencing the world for the first time.

January 30, 2021 2:44 am

Jillian S. M. Lurie

I want to hold you and have you be mine. Pure Ecstasy
flowing through my veins.
Reminding me what true peace and euphoria feels like.
My hands are warm.
My body is melting.

March 14, 2021 2:51 pm

My heart increases its beat whenever you cross my mind.
My body gravitates towards you when I see you.
My burning for you grows.

March 12th, 2021 7:16 pm

I'm currently prohibited from being in love with you.
I've never wanted to break the rules so bad.

March 20th, 2021 7:08 pm

Pretending we are together as I hold your hand.
That tragically is the closest I can get to loving you.

March 21, 2021 5:06 pm

Silly me,
For a moment in time I thought I was special to you.
I forgot for a second I'm always second best.
I'm angry he reminds me of that.
I'm nothing compared to her.
He's falling in love with her as I write.
My anxiety fills in blanks.
I can't even talk to him about it.
Thank you. I guess thank you for making me forget for a second that I could ever be important enough for it to only be me he felt.
Nice for a second really nice but you've reminded me again I'm constantly on the back burner of every man's mind.

March 23, 2021 5:14 pm

Suddenly you made me question my entire existence and fate and how you would wrap yourself into it.

March 28th, 2021 5:41 pm

I am alone again daydreaming about you.
I finally understand what all my pain was for. I'm in awe as to how special he is.
Getting used to kindness is new to me. Suddenly I am okay with my pain.
All because you're everything I've ever needed.
I found love.

April 17th, 2021 4:24 pm

Don't be too much again.
Don't put yourself in the position of wanting to change
your past.

April 27th, 2021 6:10 pm

Jillian S. M. Lurie

I shared my ideas.
He smiled.

May 3rd, 2021 4:29 pm

All my demons come out when I close my eyes in the silent dark to fall asleep.

I see my worst nightmares and anxieties inflicting on my lover and it's unfair. 4:29 thoughts.

June 15th, 2021 4:29 am

Is my life a reality that I've convinced myself to be true?

June 24, 2021 1:59 am

I haven't written in a while.
Ribs are the cage for the heart.
The heart is so wild with love.
Mom once told me healthy love lasting love takes work toxic ones don't take effort and that's the difference.
Life's starting to make more and more sense to me as time goes on.
Everyone deserves effort and time.
Toxic people don't understand that if they do spend the right effort they will never achieve a healthy relationship. You need acceptance that they don't understand this. Then you can realize their actions are not your fault. Sometimes people evolve without each other. I need to put effort, love, and hope for the return. I'm not entirely sure of the future no one ever is. I just hope with all my heart that it's with him. Life isn't fair but people can create their own luck if they try.

October 14th, 2021 2:29 am

Jillian S. M. Lurie

Life is healing.
There are beautiful things in everything.
It's your choice to focus on the bad or the good.
There is good in every bad situation.
Words I need to repeat to myself to survive.

October 19th, 2021 9:40 pm

He was sleep talking and murmured:
"I love you, baby, you're the best thing that's ever happened to me."
Little miracles everywhere.
I am so blessed to have you.
So secure.
A love redefined.
A love that defeats all others.

October 19th, 2021 10:37 pm

The healing never stops. Even when things are low.
Even when you feel stagnant and delusional.
The healing never stops.
Even when it feels stagnant.
Feeling like it's the end of the world.
Accept everything you perceive as bad about yourself.
Especially in your past.
Love that, forgive work on that. To accept is to be at peace of mind.

October 20th, 2021 at 12:24 pm

Behind closed doors a man can tear a good woman apart. Especially when he knows her heart is vulnerable to him.
Especially when he gets her alone.

October 20th, 2021 12:40 pm

You re-define a lot of things.
I couldn't ever believe I would exist for myself.
As I look at your sleep connecting with your warmth and grounding energy, I truly realize I've never had a rock until I met you.
I understand the meaning now.
It is you and I.

October 20th, 2021 1:38 pm

He brings me the kind of happiness that I find in peace and comfort.

His presence and the thought of him melt my soul into his.

Intertwining ever so harmoniously.

He brings me the calmness I feel when I'm in a field of flowers or listening to the waves crash in the ocean.

I never knew someone could bring so much feeling through my veins and my spirit.

I love him to the edge of the universe and back.

But the universe is always expanding so my love always grows. It's unmeasurable and I am happy.

November 1st, 2021 11:34 pm

Jillian S. M. Lurie

If it's meant for you, it won't be toxic.

It won't bring out your insecurities or your fears or the worst in you because it will bring peace into your life and into your heart.

If it's meant for you, it won't feel like a burden. You won't have to explain to anyone why it's not as bad as they think it is and you won't have to go to sleep wondering if you're lying to yourself because you'd be sure of it. You'd be sure that it's right for you.

If it's meant for you, it won't feel like a war. A war with yourself because you're letting it drag on or because you can't get out of it. A war with your friends because they can all see that you're suffering. If it is meant for you it wouldn't feel like a war with love because part of you knows that it shouldn't be this hard. If it's meant for you, you won't have to constantly question if it is. You won't have to look for signs or ask for advice or look for confirmation that it's right. You'd just know. It will feel like home. It will make you feel safe. It will give you one less thing to worry about. It will be healthy for you.

If it's meant for you, you won't have to chase after it. You won't have to try too hard or turn your life upside down for it to work. You won't have to lose yourself so you can keep it.

If it's meant for you, it will bring you closer to who you really are. It will enhance all the beautiful parts of you and make you more open to love, more nurturing, more compassionate and more forgiving.

If it's meant for you, it won't break your heart. There may be disappointments or letdowns or conflicts but it will never break your spirit, it will never close your heart off and it will never let you suppress your innermost feelings.

If what's meant for you doesn't come around very often, but when it does, when it's not another lesson or another mistake, when it's finally yours after everything you've endured and everything you've been through, it comes like a wave washing over you.

It feels like home.

December 7th, 2021 1:39 am

Visualize and transcend to wherever your consciousness goes.

December 13th, 2021 8:51 pm

My soul belongs to you.
You can devour me anytime.

December 25th, 2021 10:30 pm

My spiritual body felt our love connection before we even fell face first in love the first time our eyes locked.

January 13th, 2022 4:44 pm

Sometimes late at night I think about how I miss my childhood friends. Just the good memories but it's almost like a beautiful but flawed old vase that shattered on the floor after a long history of falling. It's just not worth trying to glue it together anymore. They weren't there when I needed them every time. I'm learning to understand that's okay. I just feel a bit lonely. Sometimes toxic people will put themselves so high in your mind. You think love doesn't exist anywhere else, it's their ploy to get away with anything. I'm grateful I'm intelligent enough to not look past that.

January 15th, 2022 10:38 pm

I can only forever blame myself for not getting out.
It's his fault for beating me.
My fault for staying.
My fault for giving faulty feelings for people who'd rather choke me in non-intimate ways.

January 29, 2022 10:34 pm

A poem for the dead.
All the tears I hold back, why?
I'm angry, I'm not sad.
My best friend is now bones.
So move on?
It's not easy.
She could be alive but she's not.
She took a whole part of me with her.
Everything I didn't know she knew.

I'm hoping that if I see you again it will be beautiful.
I hate the fact I need to live a whole life without your
presence.

January 29th, 2022 10:34 pm

I wish I could demolish my demons.
Just be done with them.
No one in my life deserves that.
Part of me and my mental illness reminds me every time.

February 7, 2022 1:38 am

Any moment in this life will feel wasted if I didn't spend it loving him.
He is my home.

February 9th, 2022 12:05 am

I just hope that one day I am yours to be chosen for the rest of my life.

February 9th, 2022 12:08 am

He is the lightness I feel when I'm walking through a meadow.
He is the peace at heart I crave.
He is the protector I need in my life.
He is the holder of my heart in the most tender way.
He knows what to do when I'm at my weakest.
He is the presence I crave the most.
He is the happiness I feel even on my rainiest of days.
He is my heart and my soul.

February 9th, 2022 12:10 am

Jillian S. M. Lurie

I hope he never thinks I don't love his whole being-that will be the day I will have failed.

February 9th, 2022 12:11 am

It was tonight I realized a life of pain was worth living through to have you in the end or even just for a moment.

I would bear the pain of a thousand daggers if it meant I could end up with you.

Just how fortunate am I to be here with you.

I do not care if I have been hurt in the past.

I will not fall victim to the people that hurt me, making me sad anymore. I just can't do it anymore.

I have him and I am just so forever grateful.

For that reason I have forgiven people that have hurt me in the past.

I let go of the pain I have harnessed.

February 9th, 2022 5:11 pm

When we cuddle it feels like the whole world stops and slows down for us. It suddenly feels like we are the only people to exist.
Our energies merge and I feel whole again.

February 15, 2022 10:35 am

I need to stand up to myself and my own mind.
I need to keep talking to myself in a way I would want
someone who loves me to talk to me. I need to talk to
myself how a friend would.
Especially when I'm my biggest bully.
I need to be my biggest protector.
I need to practice self-love.

February 15, 2022 11:40 am

Depression leaves me so bare sometimes.
Bare of emotion.
Bare of hunger.
Bare of desire to move.
Bare of desire to self-sabotage.
Bare of feeling like I'm still alive. I just feel nothing, nothing at all.

February 23, 2022 12:49 pm

I would've never fallen in love with my favorite part of the entire twenty four hours without cigarettes.

It's that time when the night is still everyone's sleeping the air is brisk and crisp with muffled cars in the distance. Nicotine takes any worries away instantly.

I would've never come outside so late if I didn't smoke cigarettes.

When everything is finally over.

All of the rushing of the day is done, then there's peace. There's truly nothing like it. Feeling like the world is finally slow and time doesn't feel so fast.

March 14th, 2022 2:26 pm

Jillian S. M. Lurie

It makes me sad for my mother that I cannot show her
my whole self without her not loving me.
Her pure soul just couldn't possibly handle every single
beautiful part of myself.

March 21st, 2022 10:36 pm

As I exhaled a Marlboro I realized that the secret to allowing positive energy into the same air that Negativity lies is to allow positive energy to enter where the bad ones lie.
Good wins over evil in that moment.

March 22nd, 2022 1:34 am

Therapy is for everyone who says that they aren't ready to look at themselves and change.

March 22nd, 2022 8:24 pm

Every time I was sexually assaulted in every way shape and form I thought to myself I'm that girl. Now I'm that girl that will have the baggage no one will want to carry.
For the weight will be too heavy.
For a long time I really believed that.
Then I met him.
Everything changed.
He loves me for the way that I am.
He carries my weight effortlessly.
I no longer hold resentment.
I'd go through anything to be with him in the end.

March 26, 2022 3:37 am

For the first time in a long time I actually feel lonely.
Ah, what a beautiful streak of non-loneliness.

June 2nd 2022 12:03 am

Things I've learned in my 20s now that I am almost 25 and been through so much messed up stuff:
1.Develop new habits and make them hobbies.
2. You're always right where you're meant to be in life. Everyone has their own journeys and hardships that make them grow wisdom and character.
3. It's not that serious.
4. Don't compare yourself to others.
5. Put aside any money you can a week even if it's a dollar, put it in savings or invest into a Roth IRA or stocks.
6. Meditate as often as you can. You learn the most that way and it actually improves your mental health so much.
7. Keep applying what therapy skills work for you.
8. The friends you have a hard time with sometimes people aren't meant to be in your life forever but they certainly are meant to be in your life and there for you for a certain amount of time and that's okay.
9. Sometimes leaving any type of negative relationship or negative people goes a long way as you are a product of your environment.
10. Chase your dreams if someone else worse off can do it you can too.
11. Manifest!
12. Raise your frequency.
13. Learn as much as you can about the world around you.
14. Using healthy products on your body is important.
15. Don't harness negative energy. Release it in any way you can. Run from it. Run like the wind baby.

16. That bad guy you think is the one. He is not the one. If he is hurting you he will not change. You need help.
17. Don't be afraid to ask for help.
18. Trust women.
19. Trust your intuition.
20. Don't focus on giving too much. If it is draining you. You have given away too much.

June 16th 2022 at 3:35 pm

There is no god, we are all one energy. One with the leaves, the elephants, and the same conscious energies as our biggest enemies.
There is only the universe and the space it expands into the universe is my creator.

June 20th, 2022 4:03 pm

I no longer hold onto hate and negative energy.
I feel at peace with my pain no longer giving it power.
I am untouchable by fear, hate and any low vibrational feelings.
I am safe in my home.
I thank everyone who has hurt me and helped me.
I forgive them now because without everything bad that has happened to me I wouldn't be here.
I release that pain.
I am home.
I am at ease.

July 2nd, 2022 12:10 pm

If I could ask everyone who cared for me one question
it would simply be,
"if you didn't need me would you still claim to love
me?"

July 3rd, 2022 at 9:33 pm

So torn between the future and the present. I should only focus on the here and now but my mind is too far out.

August 4th, 2022 1:41 am

The universe crushed my spirit because I needed to grow from nothing.

August 4th, 2022 2:26 am

Behind every villain is someone that made them that way.

August 14th, 2022 11:31 pm

If it's one thing I've learned in life it is you need to cut people off while you grow.

Sometimes people are sick and you can't get better with them there.

Sometimes they are contagious.

Sometimes they don't want to make you sick but they do anyway.

Sometimes they want to make you sick.

September 18th 2022 1:13 am

"You don't need to go through it alone anymore baby. I got you, it'll be okay, you are safe with me." He assured me while I crumbled in his arms on his lap. Ah, love.

September 24th, 2022 12:33 am

You are not dead.
You're everywhere around me.
Your free, reckless, beautiful soul is free now.
Now nothing and no one can hurt you.
You were blessed to be alive and I was blessed to know you. They say I'll see you again.
I feel you everywhere. You remind me of a beaming sun.
I find you everywhere down to the music that plays in the car. Your warmth was contagious.
I broke down today.
I wish you were here.

September 24th, 2022 12:36 am

The irony of loneliness is that everyone feels it all together.

October 2nd, 2022 5:50 pm

Just feeling your soul intertwined with mine feels so divine. When I'm with you I've never felt so fine.
Longing for your lust.
Longing for your kiss.
You're the only man I ever want to miss.

December 30th, 2022 10:48 pm

So much peace in the night.
No matter what goes on when the whole world is asleep.
No one can bother me, it's the safest I feel.

February 10th, 2023 2:32 pm

How would I ever be expected to be able to sleep without you for the rest of my life?

Being without your warmth in bed has been a barren loneliness that I can't explain.

I lived in such ignorance before I felt our love. Now I just simply cannot end the day without it.

February 10th, 2023 11:08 pm

I remember realizing drugs didn't kill me. I was maybe twenty two years old. I was smoking a cigarette in the dark at a hotel and cried happy tears. I realized drugs didn't kill me, that I won't die young from drugs. I fell to the ground realizing that despite my battle with wanting death to come my way sometimes at the end of the day. Life is such a rare experience and to miss out on it- that would be a true tragedy. It just made me emotional. I just sat down and finished my cigarette while I teared up. Grateful my life was spared.

February 11th, 2023 1:01 am

Everything else looks perfect, everyone else says nothing is.
Everything is so divinely perfect though.
If you really take a second to look at everything and wonder if it is truly perfect. You will see, it is.

February 21, 2023 5:33 pm

What's the key to a healthy relationship? Here's one perspective- "just gotta build" my mom once told me after I inquired: "why do toxic relationships last so long? Short euphoric ones are so short they have no issues. Some only are just right just in between. Just like you and dad?" She told me: "Healthy relationships take a lot of work, a lot of building and building takes time."

February 21, 2023 7:37 pm

Maybe it's falling apart because you need a new beginning. Things fall apart before falling together I noticed.

February 22, 2023 7:01 pm

All I wanted was to not lose someone. All I wanted was to not lose someone. All I wanted was to not lose someone.
I thought I was being careful.
Then I thought I didn't need to please.
Don't prove me wrong, you promised.

February 23rd, 2023 2:18 pm

I've gotten so good at crying sometimes you don't notice.

February 23, 2023 5:35 pm

One time when I was seventeen I was talking to my dead friend.
She told me "time moves so fast it's like you blink and you're looking up at your coffin." She didn't make it to twenty five.
She didn't even make it to adulthood.
No one I've ever met reminds me of her, not even in the slightest.
I have spent my life looking for someone remotely like her.

March 5th, 2023 3:20 pm

I took a deep breath and thought to myself he's just a man. Then I remembered they're never just a man. They all bleed the same.

March 5th, 2023 5:29 pm

Maybe it wasn't him I was afraid of. Maybe I was afraid of my abuser. Maybe I was just acting out my trauma.

March 5th, 2023 7:44 pm

I have always wondered if it satisfied others to put me down when I do make the mistakes I do in life. Even when it doesn't affect them. Even when I'm trying to lead my life with my heart more than my head. Maybe I should do the opposite. Only I have grown to love that about myself. I wish he'd love that about me too. Also to understand just things I could never say out loud. Behaviors I could never relate to because I don't hurt people like that.

March 6, 2023 5:03 pm

"Why are you suddenly so bad for me?" I thought to myself.

May 25, 2023 11:55 am

There's something about me that won't be satisfied without success. I just can't imagine not wanting more for myself. I need to pursue or be doing that or have nothing. When people are telling me it's impossible it is not enough. I just find it strange because others do it too. They say the same for themselves but find it outlandish when I talk about it seriously. Just believe in yourself and support yourself premeditating on your success. Find it when people say no. You would think five years of planning, thinking and daydreaming about what would make me happiest. It has left me with much work to be done. At the right place at the right time.

June 2, 2023 6:33 pm

Drinking alone.
Conscious mind: Sigh, he must've thought I was mental. Who knows what he could think of me? I know he loves me so much. Alcohol: It's fine.
Me: Thanks. You're right. Move on.
Can I have some more wine?

June 4th, 2023 7:54 pm

"I don't know what makes me happier than making you happy.

I don't know what makes me more depressed than making you angry.

I'm not really sure how that makes me feel.

Can you hear me?

Can you hear me?

Babe can you hear me?

Are you still awake?

It's probably better that way." I tried to tell him in his sleep.

There's so much power in thinking before you speak. Imagine if he was awake if I did make him angry. This circles back to the beginning. To be conclusive again, I just don't know how it makes me feel. I used to live for more things outside of him. That made me feel happy. I don't believe there is a problem with making someone you love happy. Nonetheless, I do believe there is something wrong with me. Hopefully, I will try to be better. Hopefully, he will not leave. Maybe since I professed those words to him while he was unconscious it will help him stay a day or two longer.

June 6th, 2023 1:07 am

Jillian S. M. Lurie

All my demons come out when I close my eyes in the silent dark to fall asleep. I see my worst nightmares and anxieties inflicting on my lover and it's unfair. 4:29am thoughts

June 7th, 2023 4:29 am

There's no reason to ever want to control your life. There's no purpose in it. There are endless outcomes in the world that are just so beyond you, so unfathomable, there's just no use caring. So stop trying to control your life and just do what you can day by day. It's the balance between doing what you want to do to make you happy and working at what you need to do to survive. That is really two key elements that are essential to life. Without it how are you truly living the life offered to you in this god forsaken world?

June 7th, 2023 12:40 pm

With loss comes great opportunity.
With pain comes great strength.
With hardship comes great joy.
You really see who your friends are to your hardships.
Your hardships will sharpen you.
Your hardships will show your darkest shadows and brightest attributes after all your pain is resolved.

June 10, 2023 10:40 pm

My dead best friend once wrote:

"Toxic Light & Mind Controlling Enigmas."
Control is but an alluring illusion.
Playing with our ghostly reflections.
As we,
Desperately search in the windows of others.
Humans
Blinded eyes dance in fragile chambers.
Embellished with sensitive strands of, Death.
Energy triples through intertwined canals. Leading to
our mystically complex psyches. Awaiting to be
warped by colorful & Colorless filters.
Interpretations.
Splashes of energies, from all promises of life
encompasses us.
Hold our hands.
Kiss our paper cheeks.
Glowing paints stain our skin. Transient fares adjust the
train tracks. Lacing our brains.
Metallic voices whisper "this way." A chance, a chance
chosen.

Raquel Ashkinazi 2015

At last, the weeds decorate MY arms. Flowers bloom
through my empty sockets. Of my eyes where
miserable
Oblivion once reigned.

Raquel Ashkinazi 2015

This is my very first book. It was written during my most vulnerable times. Through recovery, loss, the grieving process, breakups, dealing with trauma, growing into my early twenties, making progress as a writer, finding love and finally finding peace. Looking back it's hard to even imagine my mind in such a place. It feels surreal. Starting from poems and notes written during alcoholism and substance abuse triggered from my best friend's death. Healing from C-PTSD is something I will be doing my whole life. If you or someone you know is struggling with mental health and/or addiction please call for help. There are so many resources to help people come out of these places. Remember - you are worth it. No matter what phase of life you are in.

Suicide hotline call : 988

neverusealone.com 1-877-696-1996

About Me

Seven years ago, when this book started, I was convinced I would not be alive writing this About Me chapter to you.

When the poetry book began, I was in the worst place of my life and was a grieving drug addict; I did not want to make it this far many times. If you are struggling, too, my heart goes out to you.

I am happy I made it.

I'm a born-and-raised Massachusetts girl. I have also lived in Maine, California, and Colorado. I am a dyslexic writer with ADHD. I struggle with epilepsy and mental health issues too.

I have been writing my whole life. I briefly took some college courses for writing here in Massachusetts, along with English courses – in addition to some courses back in California. It has always been a dream of mine to be a writer; in fact, I *never* stopped writing.

Ever since I was a young kindergartener, I have written books and short stories. I even won poetry writing competitions when I was little! Not anything substantial but something.

I get pure enjoyment and excitement out of my life doing what I do. Out of writing books, creating worlds for others, and telling stories. I especially love telling stories around the campfire or to strangers I've just met – I love meeting people of all sorts.

I can't work because of my disability, so all I have right now are my books. Nonetheless, it has been the single best thing I have done in my life.

My granddad told me he knew it was my destiny to be a writer. He knew I was talented and gifted at it, just like he is. This book is truly my greatest achievement, and I love sharing it with you.

My routine is simply waking up, making coffee, and taking care of my two cats, two Pitbulls, and one German Shepherd. Yep, you heard me: five stinkin' cute animals!

I write all day, all night, every day. I love to spend time with great people whom I love dearly. I keep my circle small; I keep those people close to me. I am very close to my parents, too.

I live a simple life here. I discovered simplicity makes me very happy. Simplicity is the serenity I have found. I am hoping my self-help book provides the unique perspective of poetry that can help you find *your* life improvement. Just as my poetry has helped me.

Jillian S. M. L.

www.ingramcontent.com/pod-product-compliance
Lightning Source LLC
Chambersburg PA
CBHW060909120626
46553CB00001B/263